Disclaimer

Thank you for purchasing my book!
FREE AND EXCLUSIVE TO SUBSCRIBERS

YOUR FREE GIFT!

Want to become a VIP Member of our Diamonds Book Club?

Your personal development is important for us and we want to offer you exclusive access to Diamonds Book Club. You will get instant access to our VIP list with FREE BOOKS, PROMOTIONS AND GIVEAWAYS.

Enjoy your Free Books and VIP Access to Diamonds Book Club!

To your success!

https://forms.aweber.com/form/64/1045768564.htm

Emotional Intelligence

The Ultimate EQ Guide To Mastering Your Emotions and Get What You Want

(Emotional Intelligence, Life Mastery, Self Awareness)

by Emma Jones

Table of Contents

Introduction

Everyone knows someone who lights up a room when they arrive; this person seems to have a secret power, one that draws others to them, a power that paves the way for them and provides them with heaping amounts of success. The truth is, all of us have this secret power, some develop it more than others, and some of us have never developed it at all.

Don't worry, this power is no longer a secret that only some

are privy to, and this book is going to break this power down and deliver it to you fully charged and ready to go.

Your emotional intelligence is a real, honest to goodness, skill that you can improve.

Once you begin improving this skill, life will open up, and you will begin to see just how important EQ is to your happiness and success in everything you do.

For decades, people assumed that confidence was the key to success, and those who were not confident remained in the shadows, passed over, unnoticed, and ignored.

Although confidence plays a part in success, today we have a deeper understanding of the skills great leaders possess, and confidence is now explained as self-actualization achieved through self-awareness, and a list of other emotional intelligence indicators.

Great leaders, effective managers, and successful individuals from all walks of life do have something in common, excellent emotional intelligence.

The best thing about EQ is that once you improve it you will notice a change, a significant and exciting change in your daily life.

There is no reason to remain a slave to your emotions, action not reaction will get you what you desire.

There is a lot of misinformation about EQ, and even more useless information and tests to improve your EQ. EQ is measured through testing similar to the way IQ is measured through testing.

Emotional intelligence testing is gaining in popularity and cognitive neuroscience is beginning to uncover the neural mechanisms behind EQ.

Cognitive neuroscience is very interested in understanding the neural basis for human emotional intelligence.

Studies in the field of cognitive neuroscience have recently provided an even deeper understanding of the neural systems that produce and control the social and emotional processes of emotional EQ.

These processes are helping cognitive neuroscientists provide recommendations for interpreting the MSCIET (Mayer, Salovey, Caruso Emotional Intelligence Test).

The MSCIET test is only one test to measure emotional intelligence, and employers are turning more and more to these tests for hiring and promoting. It is interesting to note that emotional intelligence is now more sought after than IQ. This book will help you raise your EQ and score better if and when you need to take a test for employment. It will also strengthen your personal relationships.

After reading this book, you will have a firm understanding of what EQ is, why it is important, and how you can improve your own EQ.

Each chapter is full of facts supported by cognitive neuroscience. You can improve your EQ and become the success story you read about and dream about.

Chapter 1 – Emotional Intelligence

Emotional intelligence, EQ (Emotional Quotient), and EI, are all names for the same thing. Everyone has an EQ that some believe can be scored using a test to measure it.

IQ is scored using a standard test too, and just like EQ testing, there is a test accepted by psychology professionals and it is called the MSCIET or *Mayer, Salovey, Caruso Emotional Intelligence Test.*

Many of us have searched the internet and taking random IQ or EQ tests to gauge our intelligence/emotional intelligence. Unfortunately, these tests are not professionally approved ways of gauging emotional intelligence.

The MSCIET is professionally approved and cognitive neuroscientists are studying better and more effective ways of interpreting the results.

Now that employers are using EQ tests when hiring or promoting, it is imperative that you learn the ins and outs of

EQ. You can raise your EQ by learning about the different aspects that go into measuring EQ.

Employers know that EQ weighs heavily on creating a positive work environment and it increases worker morale.

It may seem counterintuitive to value emotions over intelligence, but there are solid reasons for this. When people respect the emotions of others they tend to get along better. When people get along, workplace morale increases and so does output and the bottom end.

If you have never considered emotional intelligence as important to success you are about to learn why it is so valued in today's world. Your personal emotional stability and awareness is only part of the whole picture.

How well you interact with others on an emotional level is now just as important as your own emotional behavior.

Of course, it is always important to know the facts. Misinformation is rampant on the internet, and credibility is important to fact finding. In this chapter, you will learn about what emotional intelligence is, and why it is important to happiness and success.

What is Emotional Intelligence

Emotional intelligence is understood as your ability to perceive nonlocal cues from an individual or group and understand the emotion that is driving the individual or group.

EQ also depends on your ability to control your emotions and effectively interact with an individual or group without interjecting your own emotional thoughts and behaviors into the situation.

High emotional intelligence gives you the ability to focus on the information you are receiving from an individual or group, and behave according to the information you have received, rather than allowing your emotions control your interaction. Some people naturally have high emotional intelligence, but those who do not can improve their EQ through learning about EQ. Once you learn what it is, why it is important, and how it affects you and everyone around you, your EQ will improve.

Why is EQ More Important to Potential Employers than IQ?

Employers are beginning to understand just how important a high EQ is. The following is a list of reasons why employers believe EQ is more important than IQ, these same statements are not accurate when measured against IQ.

- EQ determines how well employees interact with each other and customers/clients
- EQ determines how well an employee deals with stress
- EQ determines the potential for solving conflicts effectively

Employers know that happy employees are valuable employees, and emotional intelligence is now understood as the key.

In the work place, it can be difficult to reconcile the emotions of every employee, but when employers use EQ testing before hiring or promoting, they are giving themselves an advantage when looking for the employees they desire.

Emotional intelligence is shown to be a major factor in solving work place conflicts effectively. It can be difficult to resolve work place conflict when emotions are running high. Individuals with high EQ scores are shown to be better at resolving these conflicts.

High EQ is shown to be an important factor in an individual's ability deal with stress. Stressful situations are navigated better by those with a high EQ. Self-awareness is a hallmark of high EQ and self-awareness is shown as a predictor of lower stress.

Emotional intelligence measured by two types of tests. One test requires a self-assessment and self-report and the other type of test uses specific questions designed to gauge EQ. Regardless of the type of test, employers are looking for high scores and neither test measures IQ.

Not everyone in the field of psychology is comfortable with these statements. Some theories suggest that IQ plays a big role in EQ abilities. For instance, the ability to perceive and interact using nonverbal cues, or to make decisions without letting emotions play a role, has been argued in favor of both IQ and EQ.

Although these arguments do exist, there is evidence to support a high IQ does not always translate to a high EQ, but a high EQ is dependent on IQ to some extent.

Those with a high IQ do not always achieve and succeed. Some individuals with high IQ's never reach their goals, yet those with mid-range IQ's and high EQ's do reach their goals more often.

This may be because IQ only measures analytical intelligence and you do not need a high EQ to perform analytical tasks. The truth is, high IQ does not translate into success, but EQ does.

Employers are focused on EQ vs IQ because a high EQ can keep things running smoothly. It is easier for an employee with adequate EQ to diffuse arguments, lead more effectively, and interact with employees as well as customers without letting emotions dictate decisions and actions.

Many employers are using some form of EQ testing before hiring or promoting. Determining EQ can be difficult and tests do not always yield accurate results.

The reason tests do not always yield accurate results is because the measurements developed to properly score the tests is inadequate. Newer ways of measuring and scoring are making these tests more accurate.

Regardless of the exactness of the test, employers believe that these tests do predict which individuals have high EQ's.

Many progressive employers are using EQ improvement techniques and some are even hiring outside assessment groups to assess employees and work place environment for supporting a more empathetic atmosphere.

Those with high EQ's appreciate efforts to improve work place morale, and they thrive in empathetic environments. Those with a high IQ seem less likely to respond to this new type of environment, but when EQ is added to the equation, employers find it makes a difference.

Chapter 2 – EQ Ability Model and Mixed Model

EQ or EI models are different ways of understanding and improving emotional intelligence. Each model has its own particular focus and explanation of what emotional intelligence is and how it works.

Each model has something to add to your quest for improving your emotional intelligence.

Ability Model - The ability model is broken down into 4 main components. Understanding each individual ability is the first step to improving your EQ. Each of these EQ abilites can be improved and strengthened in the same way that other skills are improved.

Perceiving – Perceiving the emotional state of individuals or crowds through nonverbal cues and behaviors.

Understanding – Understanding the emotional state of individuals or crowds and understanding your own emotional state. The ability to understand the complicated interplay between your own emotions and the emotions of others.

Managing – The ability to manage your own emotions and the emotions of others to effectively achieve a goal. Positive and negative emotions can help an individual achieve a goal, managing emotions gives you the power to use both positive and negative emotions effectively.

Using – The ability to use the information you gain from perception and understanding to effectively use your emotions to your advantage rather than let them wreak havoc. When you identify your emotions, and understand them, you can use them or work to correct the behaviors they produce.

Perceiving, understanding, managing, and using the emotional state of an individual, group, or yourself is what EQ ability is all about.

When you *perceive* the emotional state of others you *understand,* it then becomes easier for you to *manage* your own emotions and *use* the information when you interact with them.

Perceiving, understanding, managing and using can be summed up in one word, empathy.

Empathy is perceiving and understanding the emotional state of someone else. You behave empathetically when you manage your own emotions and focus on the emotions of another.

When you are empathetic to others you are not ignoring your own emotional needs, you are managing them. Ignoring and managing are two completely different things.

When you manage, you acknowledge your emotions but decide to deal with them differently. You cannot ignore your emotions, they will not disappear because you refuse to acknowledge them. You must learn to manage them effectively.

People in good romantic relationships say "it is the little things that count" this statement is supported by an individual's ability to use the information they have received.

A hug at the right moment means a lot to your partner, it says you have perceived their emotional state, understand them, and are focusing on them, not your own feelings, because you know how to manage your emotions effectively.

EQ ability can help you navigate the emotional landscape of your workplace effectively. Frustration is only one of many emotions you will navigate in the workplace and your EQ ability makes a big difference.

For instance, if a co-worker is frustrated and you *perceive* their frustration and *understand* how this emotion is affecting them, it is easier to *manage* your own emotions and *use* the information to ease the situation. "I see you are working hard, is there something I can help with?" instead of, "are you finished yet?" makes a world of difference to the outcome.

Improving Your EQ Abilities

You can improve your EQ abilities; the first step is to improve control over your own emotions. If you learn to control your own emotions effectively, your EQ abilities will improve because you are no longer interacting from your emotional center.

Feelings are important, but they can be a problem when you are dealing with others; especially if your emotions dictate your actions.

Social relationships suffer when both sides are acting according to emotions. When someone is insulted, angry, frustrated or fearful, their decision making skills and social skills are diminished.

Think of a time when you felt insulted and hurt…can you remember how the other person felt?

Do you remember the conversation or interaction immediately before or after the moment you experienced the hurt from the insult? Probably not, and this is perfectly normal, the emotional upheaval that occurred blurred the rest of the interaction.

Our emotions fluctuate according to what is going on around us, or interactions we are engaged in. Emotions are important, but they can also be very disruptive. To improve your EQ abilities, you must first gain control of your own emotions through self-awareness and self-management.

Strong self-awareness and self-management give you the clarity to interact with others without dealing with your own emotions. Your perception will naturally focus on the "real" issue if you are not interjecting your emotional perception into the process.

You will understand the "real" issue if you do not have to think about why you feel the way you do, and it is easier to help others (use) the information you have gained if you do not have to deal with emotions of your own.

Mixed Model

The mixed model is a set of emotional competencies that are understood by many to improve leadership capabilities and job performance.

These competencies do not have to be naturally strong, they can be improved and perfected through study, practice and understanding of the principles.

Self-awareness – Self-awareness is understanding your own emotions, motivations, weaknesses, and strengths and understanding how they affect others. Once you are self-aware you can rely on your instincts to make decisions.

Self-regulation – Self-regulation gives you the ability to redirect emotions that are not helpful to success. Self-regulation provides the ability to adapt to change because you desire progress and achievement.

Social skills – In the mixed model, social skills are used to achieve your goals, the ability to work well with others makes it easier to utilize these relationships to achieve your desired goal.

Empathy – Accepting and considering other's emotions when making decisions

Motivation – The desire to achieve is considered an emotion that is necessary for success.

The mixed model is focused on achieving success in the workplace. Some argue that this model can bring success in all areas of life but regardless of the focus, it is a model that many adhere to. You can use this model to help you on the road to improved emotional intelligence.

Using emotions to succeed is the main drive behind the mixed model. When you identify your own emotions, drives, and desires, it is easier to make decisions that will move you forward toward your goals.

Emotions have the power to disrupt our progress or propel it forward. When strong emotions are not in line with our goals, they need to be eliminated because they can become a roadblock to achievement.

Emotional situations at work or in our private lives can support our goals or damage them. It is important to identify emotions that do not support our goals so they can be adapted or changed.

The mixed model is not much different than the ability model and both can be used to improve your emotional intelligence on many levels.

Chapter 3 – Self-Awareness and Self-Management

What is Self-Awareness?

Self-awareness is the ability to recognize your emotions and identify their effects on your behavior. When you are self-aware, you know when you are leading with your heart or your head.

Emotions are reactionary, they are triggered by everything from environment to the behavior of others, even foods can trigger emotions.

Your ability to identify your emotions and their effects on your behavior is key to improving all of the other aspects of your total EQ.

There is a big difference between action and reaction; you must now separate the two and act without reacting. When you act, you are working toward a specific aim or outcome, when you react you are behaving in response to something.

What is Self-Management?

Self-management is the ability to control your own behavior. Self-management revolves around taking responsibility for your emotions and behavior. When you become self-aware, it is easier to control your behavior.

Identifying your emotions and triggers for your emotions will give you the ability to self-manage.

When you self-manage you reduce stress because you are not ignoring your emotions or negating them, you are acknowledging them.

It is easier to deal with stressful situations, and any other situation that arises because you know how to acknowledge and put your emotions aside and deal in the moment. Self-management gives you the ability to act instead of reacting.

Action vs Reaction

Action gives you power over your behavior, reaction reduces your control over your own behavior. Self-management is all about listening, thinking, deciding and then acting.

Your emotions should always be tempered with mindfulness. Your interaction with others can incite, disturb, anger and hurt, or calm, validate, help, and defuse. Self-management gives you the choice, reacting takes away that choice.

Adapting to Change

Self-management requires flexibility, you must be able to adapt to changing situations, changing emotions, and changing environments.

 The ability to adapt to change can be strengthened through self-management.

When you are flexible your interaction with others flows naturally; others will become more open with you and this leads to conversation and understanding.

When an individual is ridged, lacking flexibility, personal relationships, work relationships, and life in general suffers. Life is all about adapting to change, the openness to change encourages others to feel at ease around you because you are less judgmental.

Although habit may seem like a good thing, it is stagnant, and life is always moving forward. Your ability to adapt is what will make you a valuable employee or best friend.

No one likes to be judged, when you are truly adaptable, you have no need to judge because judging does not change the situation, it only points fingers.

If you are truly adaptable, you can understand all sides to a story and find a solution where all sides feel validated.

Adapting to change shows you have a flexible mind, flexibility bends but does not break. Adaptability requires an open mind and an open mind is necessary in all relationships.

The ability to adapt to change also lowers stress levels. Stress is a biological reaction to unknown or challenging situations and events.

The autonomic nervous system triggers physiological changes when an individual is experiencing stress. When you are flexible and can adapt to changing situations and events, they are no longer unknown or challenging.

What is Social Awareness

Social awareness is your ability to perceive and understand social interaction. When you are socially aware you perceive and understand how a social situation can affect the emotions of those involved, and how the social situation affects you.

Social awareness will boost your EQ because your awareness includes those around you; their thoughts, feelings, and behaviors are important to you. Your social awareness involves perceiving and understanding the emotions and how those emotions affect the behavior of others.

Nonverbal Cues

Nonverbal cues are important to social awareness. Nonverbal cues provide important information about your social surroundings.

When people do not respond properly to nonverbal cues it can trigger negative responses. Nonverbal cues provide you with information about social interactions you are engaged in.

Nonverbal cues are a system of communication that does not use words. Kinesics or body language, proxemics or distance/personal space or environment/appearance, paralanguage or the use of wordless voice, and haptics or the use of touch, are all forms of nonverbal communication.

Sometimes these cues are delivered consciously, other times they are deliver unconsciously.

Perceiving and understanding nonverbal cues gives you information about a person, group, or situation, before you begin to speak.

 Knowing how to approach a social situation before you open your mouth is a great skill to have. If you are perceptive of nonverbal cues, your social interactions are smoother and social situations are easier to navigate.

Chapter 4 – Improving Your Emotional Intelligence

Improving Self-Awareness

Improving self-awareness is about connecting to your emotions, understanding what triggers them.

There are techniques you can do to increase your understanding of your emotions and to recognize what triggers them. The best way to connect with your emotions is to write them down in a journal.

Your journal is an important tool for understanding your emotions and what triggers them. You don't have to write long explanations or thoughts about your emotions unless you want to. The purpose of the journal is to give your insight into your own emotions and their triggers.

When you experience strong emotions jot them down in the journal or type them into a memo on your smart phone or tablet.

Then record the trigger for the emotion. Do this until you begin to recognize emotions and triggers when they occur. You don't have to do anything about these emotions or triggers. Self-awareness is all about recognition and understanding.

Mindfulness – Another useful way to identify your emotions and their effects on your behavior is to be mindful in the moment. Mindfulness is the ability to observe your surroundings and your thoughts in the present moment. Mindfulness supports self-awareness because you are able to recognize your emotions when they occur and this gives you the ability to manage them effectively.

Improving Self-Management

Self-awareness is about recognition and understanding, self-management is about accepting and controlling. You can manage your emotions and the behaviors they trigger and when you do, your life will change.

Emotions are real and they demand attention, you need to manage them, not ignore them.

Mindfulness Meditation – mindfulness meditation helps manage your emotions because it helps you focus on the moment and pay less attention to excessive thoughts and emotions.

Mindfulness meditation is based in Buddhist principles that will help you quiet obsessive, compulsive, emotional, and stressful thoughts, and help you focus on the moment.

This type of meditation has been shown to lower anxiety, stress, and even pain. Mindfulness meditation will help you let go of negative mental attachments. Learning this type of meditation helps learn to self-manage your emotional life.

Self-Monitoring Behavior Modification Technique – Behavior modification techniques are practiced to help you control and/or eliminate behaviors that hold you back from achieving your full potential. Once you have identified emotions and behaviors that hold you back, you can use behavior modification to change your reactions to actions.

Use your journal to identify emotions and triggers that produce behaviors you are unhappy with and create a list. Use your list to self-monitor your behavior when faced with triggers and emotions from your list.

Self-monitoring is a good way to remain self-aware and socially aware. Awareness is the first step to changing your behavior. Practicing self-monitoring will strengthen your awareness, eventually you will use that awareness to implement change.

Improving Social Awareness

Improving social awareness can be strengthened through mindfulness. Mindfulness is all about paying attention to those around you. Practice being mindful of your work environment, social environment, and personal environment.

Use mindfulness meditation to learn how to quiet your mind and be present in the moment.

When your mind is quiet and present in the moment, it will be easier for you to pay attention or be mindful of your total environment. Improved social awareness will strengthen and improve:

- Perception of nonverbal cues because you are present in the moment and paying attention to your social surroundings

- Your understanding of the emotions of others because you are not focusing on their emotions not yours

- Help you manage your emotions in social situations because you will be able to calm your thoughts and focus on the moment and not emotions that may or may not be relevant

Use self-monitoring to remain aware of your behaviors during social interactions. Social awareness involves both you and those around you. If you practice self-monitoring, you will notice the importance of your behavior when interacting with others.

Your behavior can increase negativity or decrease negativity, self-monitoring gives you the insight to make a choice instead of reacting.

Improving Social Skills

Social skills can help you get ahead and stay ahead. Good social skills are crucial to success and you can learn to improve yours with these simple tips:

- Be a good listener. When you are a good listener people enjoy your company and you become better at understanding others. It is important for success to be able to work well with others, be empathetic to the needs of others. When you include the feelings of others in your decisions they are more likely to help you achieve your goals. The best way to know what they are feeling is to listen.

- Be mindful. When you are mindful of your surroundings you are more likely to say "thank you", "please", and smile. These simple things connect you to others and let them know you care. When people know, you care about others, they are more likely to help you achieve your goals.

- Be positive in your social interactions. When you are positive people like to be around you. No one enjoys spending time with a negative person, when you are positive, others are more likely to help you achieve your goals. You don't have to go out of your way and blurt out affirmations and positive quotes, just make sure you interject a positive thought into all conversations.

Improve Motivation

Motivation ebbs and flows like a tide for many of us. Sometimes we are on fire and motivation seems to ooze from our very pores, other times we are frustrated, or experiencing other emotions that sap the motivation out from under us. Keeping motivation going, no matter what you are facing can be difficult at times. Inspiration can keep motivation strong, and inspiration can come in many forms.

- Read inspirational affirmations

- Pay attention to your passions and stay on top of current trends that relate to your passions because passion spurs motivation

- Cultivate relationships that support your dreams

- Write down thoughts that motivate you and keep them with you or better yet, type them into your memos on your smart phone

Improve Perception

Improving your perception will strengthen your professional and personal relationships. Mindfulness is one way to improve perception, another is to learn about nonverbal cues. You already understand mindfulness, so let's focus on nonverbal cues.

- Learn to read body language. Body language can tell you a slew of information about someone, including their feelings about their surroundings and you.

- Learn about proxemics. Proxemics will navigate the many different ways people experience you and your intent. Personal space is only one aspect of proxemics, learning how others perceive you and your intentions through your appearance and environment are two more aspects of proxemics.

Improve Understanding

Emotional understanding helps you use your emotions and the emotions of others to help you achieve your goals. Whey you improve your emotional understanding you will better navigate complicated emotional situations and landscapes you will encounter in your work and private life.

There are times when you should focus on your emotions, and times when you need to focus on the emotions of others to achieve the best outcome.

Conclusion

Using all of the tips and information in this book you will be well prepared to utilize your emotional intelligence to improve your life in all areas. EQ is not about ridding yourself of emotions it is about identifying them and using them effectively.

Now you have the skills you need to begin improving your EQ and your life.

Your success and happiness are achievable and using your emotional intelligence to achieve is something everyone should invest in. Now you have some insight on how emotional intelligence can help you achieve. Share your new skills so other can achieve, when you offer a hand up, others will too.

www.ingramcontent.com/pod-product-compliance
Lightning Source LLC
Chambersburg PA
CBHW071305280526
45788CB00004B/1834